The Healing Touch

Encountering the Word with Women in the Gospels

Sᴿ Margaret Mary CRSS

Sᴿ Moira CRSS

Published by
Redemptorist Publications

Illustrations: Sister Mary Stephen
Design: Lis Davis, Mo Francis

Copyright © 1999 Redemptorist Publications
A Registered Charity Limited by guarantee
Registered in England 3261721

ISBN 0 85231 190 7

Printed in Britain by Biddles Limited Guildford GU1 1DA

Redemptorist
P U B L I C A T I O N S
Alphonsus House Chawton Hampshire GU34 3HQ
Telephone 01420 88222   Fax 01420 88805
rp@redempt.org   www.redempt.org

Dedication

*To all those touched by the healing embrace of Lourdes —
especially the Sick Pilgrims and the Young Helpers of all
nationalities.*

*Any proceeds from the sale of this book will go into a fund to help
enable young people to have the experience of Lourdes.*

Contents

INTRODUCTION

"Encounter" is the essence of prayer. The Gospel stories present us with a series of encounters between Jesus and a rich variety of individuals. Each of these encounters is, in some way, a moment of prayer. Many of these moments were meetings between Jesus and women. The culture in which Jesus grew up and exercised his ministry was one in which, not unlike our own, women were in a subservient position to men. Yet any reading of any one of the four Evangelists shows us again and again the essential role of women in Jesus' mission and the great recognition that Jesus gave to each of them.

Each of these encounters helps us reach a greater knowledge of the Son of God. Far from overlooking the significance of women, Jesus endorses them repeatedly, in many cases not allowing the attempts of men to dominate, to interfere with the wealth that women bring to the fullness of his life and mission.

To pray with some of these women of the Gospel may bring us, both men and women, to a new way of seeing the world. A way of justice that moves from the survival of the fittest or the loudest, to the fullest possible human – and therefore spiritual – development for all. It is a way that sees all aspects of creation as good, God-given and worthy of reverence. Everything exists in its own right and nothing is for the abuse of the other. The feminine vision of justice brings to our world an ability to trust, a merging of thinking and feeling, a valuing of emotion, an intimacy that is controlled, merciful and of the utmost depth.

A close look at some of the women who encounter Jesus reminds us of the steadfastness, the merciful courage, the generosity and strong faith and sense of justice found in women. They do not need to be called – they seek out Christ; they give themselves to the mystery of God and bear it to others, not needing to rationalise or have it explained to them.

The circumstances in which Jesus meets the women range across a wide spectrum of situations. He is born of a woman, he debates with women, he allows women to minister to him and in turn ministers to several women himself. Indeed his own understanding of the inclusiveness and breadth of his mission is developed by a woman.

Finally, and most significantly, he chooses women to be the primary witnesses to his Resurrection and entrusts to them the passing on of this most central of events – surely the greatest affirmation.

This book seeks to encourage both women and men to contemplate some of these women in their encounters with Jesus, and in so doing to allow the femininity of their persons to develop more fully.

A change in millennium challenges us all to look anew at the values which underpin our society, to question again the accepted norms of our culture, and to renew ourselves spiritually. In looking at the models offered to us by these women, we can see the paramount importance of a new world order which recognises the centrality of Justice and Mercy and the complementarity of the male and the female, both within each one of us and within our culture. We thus have the chance to be part of the growth into complete wholeness and integrity which is God's deep desire for us all, and to make a move closer to a world where "Justice and Mercy embrace".

Sr Margaret Mary CRSS

Sr Moira CRSS

THE MEETING OF ELIZABETH AND MARY

LUKE 1:39-45 AND 57-58

Openness and Mutuality

Mary set out at that time and went as quickly as she could to a town in the hill country of Judah. She went into Zechariah's house and greeted Elizabeth. Now as soon as Elizabeth heard Mary's greeting, the child leapt in her womb and Elizabeth was filled with the Holy Spirit. She gave a loud cry and said, "Of all women you are the most blessed, and blessed is the fruit of your womb. Why should I be honoured with a visit from the mother of my Lord? For the moment your greeting reached my ears, the child in my womb leapt for joy. Yes, blessed is she who believed that the promise made her by the Lord would be fulfilled."

Meanwhile the time came for Elizabeth to have her child, and she gave birth to a son; and when her neighbours and relations heard that the Lord had shown her so great a kindness, they shared her joy.

1. Read and reread the passage reflectively.

2. Context

This is a rare example in the Gospels of an intimate moment when two women come together to give and receive openly and in full mutuality. Few words are used, yet an extraordinary depth of communication and respect are very evident.

3. Consider

● each woman has extraordinary news to give, but each remains open to the good news of the other.

● the lives of both Mary and Elizabeth have been transformed by their openness to the Spirit. Elizabeth's barrenness has become fertile, and the Virgin Mary has conceived the Son of God.

- neither woman dwells on her own glory, but both acknowledge God at work in their lives and give glory to him in true humility, recognising his merciful love.

- at this significant moment in her life, Mary has left her home and set out "in haste" to visit Elizabeth, respecting her older kinswoman.

- in turn, at a special moment in her life, Elizabeth opens her home to her younger relative for three months.

- the sensitivities of each woman go beyond words and recognise instinctively the truth and blessedness of her own and the other's situation.

- the women are happy to share the source of their joy with each other and with neighbours and friends.

4. Prayer

Pray with Mary and Elizabeth in turn, asking God to help you to be aware that he is the source of your joys and good fortune.

Be aware of moments in your life when it is difficult to put aside your own happiness to share fully in someone else's.

Pray for an increase in sensitivity so that you can listen more attentively to others.

I thank you, Lord, for the inspiration
of this Gospel story.
Help me to keep you as the focus
of my life, always mindful of the
essential part you play in all
that I do.
May I never be so involved in my
own joys or sorrows that I cannot
share those of others –
those close to home, and those
of our fellow human beings in
other parts of the world.

ANNA, THE PROPHETESS

LUKE 2:36-38

Waiting on the Lord

There was a prophetess also, Anna the daughter of Phanuel, of the tribe of Asher. She was well on in years. Her days of girlhood over, she had been married for seven years before becoming a widow. She was now eighty-four years old and never left the Temple, serving God night and day with fasting and prayer. She came by just at that moment and began to praise God; and she spoke of the child to all who looked forward to the deliverance of Jerusalem.

1. Read and reread the passage reflectively.

2. Context

Anna is one of the prophetesses who witnessed to God's will by holiness of life, by worshipping with fasting and prayer night and day and by prophesying in his name.

The situation is simply one of Jewish ceremonial, as the child Jesus is brought to the temple to be presented to the Lord.

3. Consider

● Anna was of a great age – and therefore, traditionally, a woman of wisdom. She gave her whole life to the worship of God and remained in the temple for years, waiting for the Messiah to come, confident in the prophecies of the Old Testament.

● She immediately gave thanks and praised God publicly.

● Anna knows her mission, and is quick to share her recognition with those awaiting the Saviour.

4. Prayer

Look honestly at the quality of your prayer. Is it open?

Do you wait patiently on God in readiness for his appearing?

Pray for a quietening of your spirit in prayer – for open listening and a desire to recognise the coming of God in the still small voice of silence.

Give thanks for those occasions when God has been evident in the circumstances of your life.

Pray that you will have the courage and the wisdom to know how and when to speak to others of the Lord's presence in our world.

God and Father, I am waiting for you
to show more fully your presence
in my life.
Help me to recognise you within myself
and in others.
Thank you for coming to me.
You come with your spirit of mercy and justice.
May that spirit be my guide
as I try to follow your way.

THE WEDDING AT CANA

JOHN 2:1-12

Belief and Trust

Three days later there was a wedding at Cana in Galilee. The mother of Jesus was there, and Jesus and his disciples had also been invited. When they ran out of wine, since the wine provided for the wedding was all finished, the mother of Jesus said to him, "They have no wine." Jesus said, "Woman, why turn to me? My hour has not come yet." His mother said to the servants, "Do whatever he tells you." There were six stone water jars standing there, meant for the ablutions that were customary among the Jews: each could hold twenty or thirty gallons. Jesus said to the servants, "Fill the jars with water," and they filled them to the brim. "Draw some out now," he told them, "and take it to the steward." They did this; the steward called the bridegroom and said, "People generally serve the best wine first, and keep the cheaper sort till the guests have had plenty to drink; but you have kept the best wine till now."

This was the first of the signs given by Jesus: it was given at Cana at Galilee. He let his glory be seen, and his disciples believed in him. After this he went down to Capernaum with his mother and the brothers, but they stayed there only a few days.

1. Read and reread the passage reflectively.

2. Context

This is another story which is only found in John's gospel, and is the first of Jesus' outward "signs" which lead people to believe that he is the Messiah. A wedding in Palestine was a very notable event and the festivities would last for several days – for a week, a wedding couple would keep open house, and this week of joy was one of the supreme occasions of happiness for any couple. It is important to understand this context, because it explains why running out of wine was so significant. To run out of wine would be a severe embarrassment to the newly-wedded couple.

3. Consider

● Mary is quietly attentive to the practicalities of the situation, and notices the potentially embarrassing situation which may arise if they run out of wine. Having pointed this out to Jesus, she takes a back seat and trusts that he will deal with the situation in a merciful way.

● Mary knows that Jesus' compassion will embrace the difficulties threatening to spoil the joyful occasion.

● Mary's supreme confidence in Jesus. His initial response to her is not encouraging. Yet she tells the servants to do whatever Jesus asks of them. She continues to believe in him even when she does not understand what he is going to do.

● it is Mary's gentle encouragement and persistence which support Jesus towards his Father's will, in this miracle at Cana.

4. Jesus' response

Jesus' response to his mother is easily misinterpreted because of the words used in translation – "Woman, why turn to me?" In fact, his form of address "Woman" is far from discourteous. It is the same word ("Gunai") which he uses on the cross as he hands his mother into the care of John. Said gently to a mother, it implies great love and respect. What he is telling her is that he will handle the situation and that she must not worry.

His next words – "My hour has not come yet" – are a clear indication that Jesus' response to all the situations in his life will be to act in accordance with his Father's wishes.

As he momentarily hesitates to begin his public ministry, his mother's gentle insistence encourages him. This first miracle is, in fact, in accordance with the will of his Father.

Jesus' response to the situation can now be seen on two very different levels. Firstly, he wanted to save a humble Galilean family from hurt and humiliation. He brought forth his power in sympathy and kindness.

Secondly, Jesus' power and the glory of God are manifested – it is indeed a "glorious" occasion.

5. Prayer

Put yourself in Mary's position. Allow her belief and trust in her son to become real in your heart. Think over those situations in your life which you need to hand over to God, and do so in trust, confident of his mercy.

Pray that Mary's trust and faith in Jesus will be real for people who are in demanding circumstances in the world. Ask God to show them real signs of his love manifest in their lives.

Father in Heaven, your son came to do
your will.
His mother was instrumental in your great plan.
Thank you for sending Jesus
to show us the way to you.
Thank you for Mary who is the perfect
woman and mother
Help me to believe and hope in you,
and to come closer to your son,
Jesus, and his mother.

WOMAN AT THE WELL

JOHN 4:5-30

Conversion and Mission

On the way he came to the Samaritan town called Sychar, near the land
that Jacob gave to his son Joseph. Jacob's well is there and Jesus, tired by the
journey, sat straight down by the well. It was about the sixth hour. When a
Samaritan woman came to draw water, Jesus said to her, "Give me a
drink." His disciples had gone into town to buy food. The Samaritan woman
said to him, "What? You are a Jew and you ask me, a Samaritan, for a
drink?" – Jews, in fact, do not associate with Samaritans. Jesus replied:

"If only you knew what God is offering
and who it is that is saying to you:
Give me a drink,
you would have been the one to ask,
and he would have given you living water."

"You have no bucket, sir," she answered "and the well is deep; how could
you get this living water? Are you a greater man than our father Jacob who
gave us this well and drank from it himself with his sons and his cattle?"
Jesus replied:

"Whoever drinks this water
will get thirsty again;
but anyone who drinks the water that I shall give
will never be thirsty again:
the water that I shall give
will turn into a spring inside him,
welling up to eternal life."

"Sir," said the woman "give me some of that water, so that I may never get
thirsty and never have to come here again to draw water."
"Go and call your husband," said Jesus to her, "and come buck here." The
woman answered, "I have no husband." He said to her, "You are right to

say, 'I have no husband'; for although you have had five, the one you have now is not your husband. You spoke the truth there."
"I see you are a prophet, sir" said the woman. "Our fathers worshipped on this mountain, while you say that Jerusalem is the place where one ought to worship." Jesus said:

> "Believe me, woman, the hour is coming
> when you will worship the Father
> neither on this mountain nor in Jerusalem.
> You worship what you do not know;
> we worship what we do know;
> for salvation comes from the Jews.
> But the hour will come – in fact it is here already
> when true worshippers will worship the Father
> in spirit and truth:
> that is the kind of worshipper
> the Father wants.
> God is spirit,
> and those who worship
> must worship in spirit and truth."

The woman said to him, "I know that Messiah – that is, Christ – is coming; and when he comes he will tell us everything."
"I who am speaking to you," said Jesus, "I am He."
At this point his disciples returned and were surprised to find him speaking to a woman, though none of them asked, "What do you want from her?" or, "Why are you talking to her?" The woman put down her water jar and hurried back to the town to tell the people, "Come and see a man who has told me everything I ever did; I wonder if he is the Christ?"
This brought people out of the town and they started walking towards him.

1. Read and reread the passage reflectively.

2. Context
There has been mounting controversy in Judaea surrounding Baptism and the person of John the Baptist, so Jesus has decided to leave that country and return to Galilee, taking the shortest route through Samaria.

At this time and in this place it would have been unheard of for a rabbi to speak with women in public or for a Jew to request water from a Samaritan. Although there was this ill-feeling between Jews and Samaritans, this well in Samaria where Jesus stops to rest and have a drink, was full of Jewish memories. It was traditionally Jacob's well and the place of Joseph's burial. The well was so deep that nobody could get water from it without a bucket. In this passage the time is midday and the heat is at its greatest. There was water available at Sychar, but it is perhaps an indication of the level of the woman's disrepute that she should have to walk more than half a mile out of town in the heat to get her water.

3. Consider

● this story contains significant revelations about Jesus, Eternal Life and the Father in Heaven. The focus for these revelations is a woman.

● as a woman, already a victim of abuse and discrimination amongst her own people on account of her ill-repute, she is able to lay aside her own hurts and prejudices in order to listen to Jesus, whom she quickly recognises to be either a "prophet" or even perhaps the Christ.

● although the woman needs Jesus to explain to her very carefully and patiently, she is very quick to respond to the essential offer that Jesus is making her, of the true and living water.

● it is in the presence of Jesus that the woman is able to face herself and her history and cease her evasions. In recognising the power of Jesus, she awakens both to herself and to her need of God. There is a sudden realisation that life, as she has been living it, will not do. This realisation comes from the revelation of herself in the presence of Christ.

● despite her wayward life, the woman has an intuitive grasp of the spiritual essence of what Jesus is saying and can lead him to say to her: "I who am speaking to you ... I am He." Equally quickly she moves on to mission as she shares her experiences with the very people of her own town who must have known the history of her dissolute life. Having shared with them, she is instrumental in bringing them to Jesus.

4. Jesus' response

Jesus is untroubled by scruples based on traditional prejudice.
He does not hesitate to use Samaritan utensils which Jews would have considered as unclean.

He is prepared to engage in an open and intimate conversation with someone who is not only a Samaritan but a woman as well – and a woman of ill-repute. He is friendly and sympathetic to the woman; not hostile or critical. Yet he confronts the realities of the woman's life head on.

He is patient in explaining who he is and what the water is that he offers, while at the same time displaying the reality of his humanity in his weariness and thirst.

Jesus is sensitive and intuitively assesses what encouragement and explanations the woman needs. He starts with the mundane reality of his own physical thirst, and having engaged her, he is able to lead her step by step into a significant understanding of God as the quencher of spiritual thirst.

Jesus' gaze is not merely a kind, compassionate one – it sears through layers of the woman's life experience and attempted evasions, and yet it does so in such a way that ultimately brings her to peace, faith and integrity as she confronts the justice and mercy of God.

5. Prayer

In praying with the Samaritan woman, become aware of the fullness of God's mercy – open even the darkest corners of your life to the loving and penetrating gaze of God, confident of his love and forgiveness.

In your prayer accept from God the living, healing water of his life, asking him for the strength to live by his spirit and his truth.

Lord, you were weary and thirsty
when you met this woman.
You gave of your very best to her, a woman,
a Samaritan woman of disrepute, and
she was open to receive.
Help me to be open to your approach.
Help me to understand what you
are saying to me and to follow
where you are leading.
I thank you for the kindness
and forgiving healing I have already received
from you and I hold up to you
those most in need of your presence
in their hearts.

THE WIDOW OF NAIN

LUKE 7:11-17

Jesus' kindly regard
for a suffering woman

Now soon afterwards he went to a town called Nain, accompanied by his disciples and a great number of people. When he was near the gate of the town it happened that a dead man was being carried out for burial, the only son of his mother, and she was a widow. And a considerable number of the townspeople were with her. When the Lord saw her he felt sorry for her. "Do not cry," he said. Then he went up and put his hand on the bier and the bearers stood still, and he said, "Young man, I tell you to get up." And the dead man sat up and began to talk, and Jesus gave him to his mother. Everyone was filled with awe and praised God saying, "A great prophet has appeared among us; God has visited his people." And this opinion of him spread throughout Judaea and all over the countryside.

1. Read and reread the passage reflectively.

2. Context

This story has links with the Old Testament stories of raising from the dead, and with the other two New Testament stories of Jesus bringing the dead back to life: Jairus' daughter and the raising of Lazarus.

There is a clear progression. Jairus' daughter, according to Mark and Luke, is seriously ill, and according to Matthew has just died. The widow's son here is dead and his funeral is taking place. Lazarus has already been four days dead in the tomb. The culmination of these stories clearly comes in the Resurrection of Jesus himself.

This story is a straightforward miracle, motivated by Jesus' heartfelt compassion for a woman, a mother and a widow who has lost her only son.

3. Consider

● the scene. A funeral, a funeral procession, a mother with no husband, no other children, accompanied by the townspeople. The woman weeps.

● the change in atmosphere when Jesus, moved by compassion, shows the fullness of his mercy and brings the son back to life.

● for the first time in Luke's Gospel, Jesus is referred to as "Lord" (ho kyrios) – a title which is the Divine Name, Yahweh. It is used here to initiate Jesus' role as having power over life and death, and to foreshadow his own resurrection, when he becomes Lord (ho kyrios) in the fullest sense of the word.

● the links between this story and Elijah's raising from the dead the only son of a widow in 1 Kings 17:17-24. The words of the crowd: "God has visited his people" show that connections are being made between Jesus and the Messiah promised in the Old Testament.

● the emphasis on the only son. Christ was the only son of God. Again this links this story to the death and resurrection of Christ.

4. Jesus' response

Jesus was accompanied by his disciples and a large crowd and yet he paid attention to this funeral procession and in particular to the woman at the centre of it – a mother.

Jesus' concern throughout is for the woman, not for her son. In one translation: "his heart went out to her". In this particular instance the woman has not even had to ask Jesus for his mercy: her predicament itself brings forth the power of God, mediated through Jesus' human compassion.

Having restored the son to life, Jesus makes direct contact with the woman in handing back to her the son she mourned.

5. Prayer

Focus on the boundless mercy of God shown here in the full and instinctive compassion of Jesus for a woman in deep sorrow.

Ask God to enlarge the trust you have in him so that you know he loves and cares for you and will be with you in your moments of deepest sorrow, even when you have no word with which to call on him.

Pray that your heart will be sensitive to others in need and that your response will be as compassionate as Jesus'.

Pray in particular for all those people in the world whose circumstances push them to despair, asking God to be present in their lives.

Lord, I thank you and I praise you
for the loving compassion you show me.
Help me to share in that compassion for others.
Help me to recognise situations of deep distress,
and bring life to them
using the same power that you used
to bring the Widow's son to life again.
Show your loving mercy
to those across the world
who suffer injustice.

THE WOMAN WITH A HAEMORRHAGE

LUKE 8:43-48

Courage in Faith

*Now there was a woman suffering from a haemorrhage for twelve years,
whom no one had been able to cure. She came up behind him and touched
the fringe of his cloak; and the haemorrhage stopped at that instant. Jesus
said, "Who touched me?" When they all denied that they had, Peter and his
companions said, "Master, it is the crowds around you, pushing." But Jesus
said, "Somebody touched me. I felt that power had gone our from me."
Seeing herself discovered, the woman came forward trembling, and falling
at his feet explained in front of all the people why she had touched him and
how she had been cured at that very moment. "My daughter," he said, "your
faith has restored you to health; go in peace."*

1. Read and reread the passage reflectively.

2. Context

This passage comes as an interruption in the story of the raising of Jairus'
daughter.

This is an unusual episode since initially the woman has no intention of
making direct contact with Jesus on a personal level. Her faith and her
desperation tell her that the touch of his garment alone will bring the healing.
Notice that Jesus insists on a personal encounter with the woman, for meeting
Jesus face to face is part of the healing process.

3. Consider

● the woman has been ill for many years, has consulted many physicians and
could not be healed by anyone. Yet she still hopes for a cure.

- in her culture, her condition would have classed her as a social outcast, worthy only of stoning, yet she instinctively felt drawn to Jesus, despite the dangers.

- she appears to be alone, is afraid and meets with difficulty in getting close to Jesus.

- in her desperation all her instincts lead her to believe that the touch of Jesus alone could bring her healing: she is convinced of the power of his mercy.

- despite the fact that Jesus is on his way elsewhere, her faith is strong enough to risk the interruption.

- finding herself healed and discovered by Jesus, the woman moves quickly to testify publicly to her humiliating affliction and to Jesus' healing power in her life.

4. Jesus' Response

Jesus alone has the sensitivity to feel and recognise the woman's touch and cry for healing – a specific touch amidst pushing crowds. The mere sincerity of her wordless touch called forth his healing power.

Jesus affirms that it is the woman's faith which has brought her healing and peace.

5. Prayer

Reflect on any situations in your life at the moment which cause you concern for yourself or for others.

Try to identify with the woman and pray with her through her story and through yours.

Ask God to bring the woman's faith, courage and love of Jesus into your life.

Reflect on the healing touch of Jesus – so sought after and so powerful. Ask God for the sensitivity to see where you can minister his healing touch to others. Pray that you find ways of sharing God's mercy.

Spend time holding up before the Lord those situations on which you have reflected.

Lord, I pray for healing –
healing for myself and for those
dear to me.
Increase my faith in your power
to affect my life.
May your healing touch be
experienced in areas of conflict
in the world.
I praise and thank you for
your presence amongst us.

THE CANAANITE WOMAN

MATTHEW 15:21-28

Breaking down Barriers

Jesus left that place and withdrew to the region of Tyre and Sidon. Then out came a Canaanite woman from the district and started shouting, "Sir, Son of David, take pity on me. My daughter is tormented by a devil." But he answered her not a word. And his disciples went and pleaded with him. "Give her what she wants," they said, "because she is shouting after us." He said in reply, "I was sent only to the lost sheep of the House of Israel." But the woman had come up and was kneeling at his feet. "Lord," she said, "help me." He replied, "It is not fair to take the children's food and throw it to the housedogs." She retorted, "Ah yes, sir; but even housedogs can eat the scraps that fall from their master's table." Then Jesus answered her, "Woman, you have great faith. Let your wish be granted." And from that moment her daughter was well again.

1. Read and reread the passage reflectively.

2. Context
This is one of the rare encounters of Jesus with a Gentile, and the scene takes place in a remote area outside Jesus' own immediate home country. It is of significance that the woman is a Canaanite, for the Canaanites were traditional enemies of the Chosen People, and within that culture embodied all that was wicked and godless.

3. Consider

● the woman's bravery.
  She is neither resentful nor deterred by Jesus' initial lack of response and subsequent positive discouragement. With admirable tenacity she persists in pleading with Jesus to save her daughter. Her example is one of devotion, patience and unfaltering determination.

- her humility and devotion to her daughter.
  She identifies so completely with her daughter's condition that she asks Jesus to have pity on her, the mother and to help her. She knows that if he responds to her pleas, her daughter will be cured, so perfect is her compassion.

- the woman's faith and courage.
  She, a Gentile, is prepared to challenge Jesus to extend his mission beyond the House of Israel. She argues from the standpoint of justice – that Jesus' mission was not limited to particular groups in society.

4. Jesus' response

In Jesus' understanding of his identity and his mission, the Canaanite woman plays a unique and significant part.

In this short incident he moves from believing that his mission was only to the House of Israel to an inclusive and fuller appreciation of the scope of his ministry. It is the woman's persistence and faith which have enlarged his understanding.

At the end of the episode he compassionately honours the woman's great faith and heals her daughter.

5. Prayer

With the Canaanite woman, look prayerfully at relationships entrusted to you, asking God for a compassion which is not possessive nor exclusive, for a humility which puts the other first.

Pray for the \faith and courage to persist in placing yourself and those you love before Jesus, trusting in his love, mercy and healing.

*Lord, you inspired the Canaanite
woman with great vision,
faith and courage.
I pray today for my own needs,
thanking you for all the graces
you have given me already.
And I pray for all those people who
need your inspiration to help
them break down the barriers of
injustice and cruelty in their
lives and in the lives of
others.*

MARTHA AND MARY

LUKE 10:38-42

Embracing Complementarity

In the course of their journey he came to a village, and a woman named Martha welcomed him into her house. She had a sister called Mary, who sat down at the Lord's feet and listened to him speaking. Now Martha who was distracted with all the serving said, "Lord, do you not care that my sister is leaving me to do the serving all by myself? Please tell her to help me." But the Lord answered: "Martha, Martha," he said, "you worry and fret about so many things, and yet few are needed, indeed only one. It is Mary who has chosen the better part; it is not to be taken from her."

1. Read and reread the passage reflectively.

2. Context

This well-known passage is open to a range of interpretations, some of which limit the important truths mediated by these women. The attitudes of Mary and Martha need not be seen in opposition, but rather each woman presents a facet of the worthy entertaining of Christ. We are called to honour both facets in ourselves and in others. Martha's problem is simply that at that moment she could not accept the validity of Mary's stance.

3. Consider

● Mary's ease and comfort as she honours the Master and listens attentively to his teaching.
  "Blessed are those who hear the Word of God and put it into practice."

● Mary's intuitive grasping of the moment. Jesus has come as Master and Mary receives him as such.

● Martha's recognition that as the elder sister she must honour her guest and receive him in practical ways.

- in her desire to meet the practical demands of hospitality in as efficient a way as possible, Martha has lost sight of the essence of the situation. She becomes agitated and anxious and so loses her peace.

- unable to accept Mary's welcome of Jesus, Martha becomes hostile to both her guest and her sister.

4. Jesus' response

Jesus responds clearly but affectionately to Martha's agitation. He calls her name twice, showing his concern for her anxiety.

He does not rebuke her, but reminds her that Mary's attentive listening is an essential part of ministry.

Jesus attempts to help Martha to understand that each person can have a valid position – that justice demands that each is allowed to be herself and that each values the other. Martha is being challenged to approach her sister with mercy rather than resentment.

5. Prayer

In praying with this story, become aware of the Mary and Martha in your own life. Are both present and in balance?

Do you reverence Martha and Mary equally in yourself and in others?

In prayer, ask God to help you to integrate these different ways of welcoming Jesus and others into your life. Pray that you will never allow either to eliminate the other from your life.

Thank you, Father, for this vision of
different ways of welcoming you
into my life.
May I become more aware of my
different responses to others, and
reverence their needs with the
sensitivity of your son.
I pray especially for a growth in
understanding of how to embrace difference.
I pray to be fully involved in building
a world based on your values of respect
and mutual love.

THE HEALING OF THE CRIPPLED WOMAN ON THE SABBATH

LUKE 13:10-17

Fidelity though years of suffering

One Sabbath day he was teaching in one of the synagogues, and a woman was there who for eighteen years had been possessed by a spirit that left her enfeebled; she was bent double and quite unable to stand upright. When Jesus saw her he called her over and said, "Woman, you are rid of your infirmity" and he laid hands on her. And at once she straightened up, and she glorified God. But the synagogue official was indignant because Jesus had healed on the Sabbath, and he addressed the people present. "There are six days," he said, "when work is to be done. Come and be healed on one of those days and not on the Sabbath." But the Lord answered him. "Hypocrites!" he said. "Is there one of you who does not untie his ox or his donkey from the manger on the Sabbath and take it out for watering? And this woman, a daughter of Abraham whom Satan has held bound these eighteen years – was it not right to untie her bonds on the Sabbath day?" When he said this his adversaries were covered with confusion, and all the people were overjoyed at all the wonders he had worked.

1. Read and reread the passage reflectively.

2. Context
This is Jesus' final appearance in the synagogue in Luke's Gospel. There have already been several instances where Jesus' actions on the Sabbath have raised questions and objections. This is one such instance. The Pharisaic Jews are attempting to exploit Jesus' compassionate actions and to expose him as acting in contradiction to God's law with regard to the Sabbath.

Strict interpretation of Rabbinical law at this time would have forbidden the tying and loosing of knots on the Sabbath.

3. Consider

- the courage and faith of the woman. After eighteen years of Satanic bondage, and her obvious physical deformity, a deformity that would have been generally recognised as being a result of sin, she is still going to the synagogue. Over these long years she had remained ready to believe that God will act in her life.

- the simplicity of the healing process. Jesus sees her, calls her and says: "You are rid of your infirmity." He lays his hands on her. The woman is a receiver, and her disposition allows her simply to receive.

- the woman's first and immediate response to her healing: "She glorified God." She recognises the presence of God and she turns at once to him to give thanks and praise.

- the concept of "being bound" in this story.
  The woman has been bound by Satan for eighteen years, and her very presence in the synagogue suggests that she is aware of her condition and of its source. Her situation is so extreme that she cannot even find the words to plead to Jesus for healing – nor does she need to. Her openness itself calls forth Jesus' compassion and healing touch.
  The synagogue official and his supporters are also bound. Bound by Rabbinical law, and so bound that they are blind to those things that are beyond and above the law.

- in contrast to Jesus' compassionate observation and the woman's openness, these people are blind to the very action which could have revealed their Messiah to them. Someone who frees one of their own people from Satanic bondage on the Sabbath can only be the one who is himself the Lord of the Sabbath.

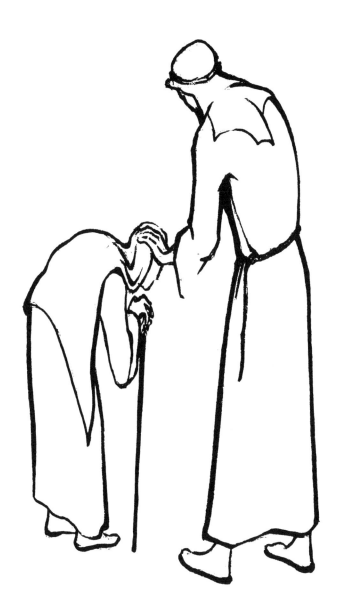

4. Jesus' response

This story is another example of Jesus' merciful regard for the unfortunate and for women. Yet again, Jesus is the one who takes the initiative in the episode. He notices the woman, calls to her and heals her without being asked in words to do so.

Jesus makes it clear that when the Kingdom of God overtakes the kingdom of Satan, laws such as those regulating the Sabbath are obsolete, and that real justice must prevail. In fact, a work of mercy such as this justly belongs to the Sabbath as much, or even more, than to any other day, because it is a work of God and it fulfils the meaning of the Sabbath rather than abuses it.

Jesus' response is strong, "...was it not right to untie her bonds...?", suggesting that liberation from Satan is a necessary work which has to be done by anyone who belongs to the reign of God, regardless of the law.

5. Prayer

Look at the woman's situation: her faith, her courage, her shame, her wordless acceptance of Jesus in her life and her ultimate joy when God takes the place of Satan in her spirit.

Ask God to help you to reflect openly on whatever is binding you at the present time, praying that you may have the courage to place your situation in God's healing hands. Allow him to free you from any blindness or hypocrisy which prevents you from serving him and other fully.

Lord Jesus, you brought this woman wholeness
and the justice of your Father's Kingdom.
Heal my blindness,
my narrow vision,
my self-centred spirit,
so that I may praise you,
your Father and your Spirit,
and bring your mercy
and your healing to others.

THE LOST DRACHMA

LUKE 15:8-10

Resolute Searching

Or again, what woman with ten drachmas would not, if she lost one, light a lamp and sweep out the house and search thoroughly till she found it? And then, when she had found it, call together her friends and neighbours? "Rejoice with me," she would say "I have found the drachma I lost." In the same way, I tell you, there is rejoicing among the angels of God over one repentant sinner."

1. Read and reread the passage reflectively.

2. Context
This story is proper to Luke's Gospel and comes as one of three parables intended to show the searching love of God and the thoroughness with which he pursues his plan to save.
This particular one of the three, which has a woman as the subject, also illustrates particular womanly characteristics.

3. Consider

● how important the lost coin is for the woman. She is poor and this coin represents a tenth of her resources.

● having lost her coin, she takes responsibility herself for its loss, and determines to find it rather than immediately appealing for charity from others.

● the woman's determination and her thoroughness. It is dark, but she swept the whole house in every corner.

● the woman's optimism in spite of her poverty. She searches believing that she can find.

● having found the coin, she shares her joy with those around her, asking them to rejoice with her.

4. Jesus' response

Jesus admires the woman's tenacity and compares her joy to the rejoicing in Heaven when a sinner repents.

5. Prayer

Ask God to help you in your moments of loss and discouragement. Pray that in times of refreshment and joy, you will want to share the rejoicing with those around you.

Lord, you search me and you know me.
I pray that I may have this woman's
hope and perseverance in times of difficulty.
May I rejoice when my hopes are fulfilled
and never forget to thank you
for your loving care of me.
Together with you, I pray in joy
at the repentance of sinners.
May I always remember my need
for your forgiveness.

THE ADULTEROUS WOMAN

JOHN 8:1-11

Justice and Mercy Embrace

At daybreak he appeared in the Temple again; and as all the people came to him, he sat down and began to teach them.
The scribes and Pharisees brought a woman along who had been caught committing adultery; and making her stand there in full view of everybody, they said to Jesus, "Master, this woman was caught in the very act of committing adultery; and Moses has ordered us in the Law to condemn women like this to death by stoning. What have you to say?"
They asked him this as a test, looking for something to use against him. But Jesus bent down and started writing on the ground with his finger. As they persisted with their question, he looked up and said, "If there is one of you who has not sinned, let him be the first to throw a stone at her." Then he bent down and wrote on the ground again. When they heard this they went away one by one, beginning with the eldest, until Jesus was left alone with the woman who remained standing there. He looked up and said, "Woman, where are they? Has no one condemned you?"
"No one, sir" she replied.
"Neither do I condemn you," said Jesus "go away, and don't sin any more."

1. Read and reread the passage reflectively.

2. Context

This is part of a concerted effort by the scribes and Pharisees to gather information which will discredit Jesus. They use this woman and her situation to test Jesus giving him alternatives which they consider will compel him to condemn himself. The passage throws light on different attitudes to people. We are shown the attitude of the scribes and Pharisees, and we are shown Jesus' attitude, and through him, the attitude of the Father to a sinner. The point of the story is not that sin is of no importance, nor that God does not punish sin. Rather it emphasises the way in which God extends mercy to sinners so that they will turn from their sins.

It is an uncluttered example of the embrace of justice and mercy in Jesus' treatment of the woman.

3. Consider

● how the woman is caught in a trap laid by the scribes and Pharisees. She is an unwitting pawn in their game, and they do not hesitate to take advantage of her vulnerability as they expose her to public shame.

● those who seek to outwit and abuse others in this situation are left humiliated in the malice of their project, once they are challenged to examine the quality of their own lives.

● the tension between the legalism of the scribes and Pharisees and the bountiful mercy of Jesus who seeks a justice which transcends mere legalism.

● the woman's feelings as her accusers began to drift away from the scene shamefully. Having been defended by Jesus, the woman is moved to listen bravely to his judgement. He will not pass judgement on her, but his command, to go and sin no more, is a lifetime's challenge, one which could inspire her to a new life in God.

4. Jesus' response

Jesus refuses to deal with case merely as a legal matter, but treats it practically and mercifully. He asks people to examine their own consciences, before proclaiming that they are worthy to sit in judgement on others.Jesus is not to be outwitted or out-manoeuvred by his critics, and he uses the occasion to extend his justice and mercy to a sinner.

Jesus' forgiveness is not light and easy, as if the sin did not matter. He defers sentence, giving her a second chance. He is concerned with her potential, with her future rather than with her past.

The fundamental difference between Jesus' response and that of the scribes and Pharisees is that the scribes and Pharisees live their lives seeking to condemn, whereas Jesus lives his looking for opportunities to forgive.

5. Prayer

With this woman, pray in thanksgiving for God's all-embracing forgiveness – for his attitude to us of searching for reconciliation, regardless of our intransigence and the magnitude of our sin.

Open your life to God and allow him to warn you and to challenge you to a new life. Be confident of his forgiveness, even when you find it difficult to forgive yourself.

Ask God to extend his manifold forgiveness to those who do not even know their need of it.

Pray that you may never take the legalistic and judgmental standpoint of the scribes and Pharisees, but may always embrace a fuller understanding of the justice and mercy of God.

"Forgive us our trespasses as we forgive those
who trespass against us."
Thank you, Jesus, for the mercy with
which you embrace me.
Keep me open to receive it.
I ask your pardon for the time I have
condemned others when I have so
much to be forgiven.
Your treatment of this woman gives me
a pattern for my life.
Be with me as I try
to live in your spirit.

THE WIDOW'S MITE

MARK 12:41-44

Total Giving

He sat down opposite the treasury and watched the people putting money into the treasury, and many of the rich put in a great deal. A poor widow came and put in two small coins, the equivalent of a penny. Then he called his disciples and said to them, "I tell you solemnly, this poor widow has put more in than all who have contributed to the treasury; for they have all put in money they had left over, but she from the little she has put in everything she possessed, all she had to live on."

1. Read and reread the passage reflectively.

2. Context

This story comes in sharp contrast to what has preceded it. Jesus has been castigating those whose religion was worn on the outside and did not reflect their inner spirit. He has made a series of charges against the scribes who were known for their flowing robes and their desire to be recognised with great respect.

The story of the widow now comes as a sign of hope at the end of Jesus' ministry. She represents "the Way" that Jesus' followers are to take if they are to be worthy of the name of Christian.

3. Consider

● the link here between giving and sacrifice.
The widow's total generosity involves her in sacrifice. Real generosity gives until it hurts.

● the woman gives both her coins. She, who is alone, takes the risk of losing everything she has.

● the fact that Jesus draws attention to the need for a just response to different levels of giving, using the widow's level as the measure.

4. Jesus' response

Jesus clearly attaches great importance to this type of generosity. Jesus and his Father do not focus attention on the intrinsic value of a gift; rather they measure the worth of an offering in terms of the sacrifice involved. This concept of total self-giving is shortly to reappear as the essence of Jesus' determination to do the will of his Father on Calvary.

Jesus does not condemn those who give more circumspectly than the widow, but he draws attention to the fact that they give of their surplus, whereas the widow's total gift is of a different quality altogether – she gives everything she has.

5. Prayer

Reflect honestly on whether your giving is in the same spirit as the widow's or is more akin to that of the others who gave "of the money they had left over". Ask God for the strength to give fully of yourself, of your time and of what you have, to situations into which he has drawn you.

Consider how much of yourself and your time you put aside to pray.

Father in Heaven,
help me to be generous –
generous in practical ways
and generous too in the giving of myself.
On his cross, your son showed me
what real self-giving entails.
Give me the courage and perseverance
that I need to follow your way.

Mary and Martha's Concern over the Death of Lazarus

John 11:20-34

Faith in Grief

When Martha heard that Jesus had come she went to meet him. Mary remained sitting in the house. Martha said to Jesus, "If you had been here, my brother would not have died, but I know that, even now, whatever you ask of God, he will grant you." "Your brother", said Jesus to her, "will rise again." Martha said, "I know he will rise again at the resurrection on the last day."
Jesus said:

> *"I am the resurrection.*
> *If Anyone believes in me,*
> *even though he dies he will live,*
> *and whoever lives and believes in me*
> *will never die.*
> *Do you believe this?"*

"Yes, Lord", she said, "I believe that you are the Christ, the Son of God, the one who was to come into this world."
When she had said this, she went and called her sister Mary, saying in a low voice, "The Master is here and wants to see you." Hearing this, Mary got up quickly and went to him. Jesus had not yet come into the village; he was still at the place where Martha had met him. When the Jews who were in the house sympathising with Mary saw her get up so quickly and go out, they followed her, thinking that she was going to the tomb to weep there.
Mary went to Jesus, and as soon as she saw him she threw herself at his feet, saying, "Lord, if you had been here, by brother would not have died." At the sight of her tears, and those of the Jews who followed her, Jesus said in great distress, with a sigh that came straight from the heart, "Where have you put him?"

1. Read and reread the passage reflectively.

2. Context

This extract comes from the longer story of the raising of Lazarus, and focuses on Jesus' interaction with Mary and Martha.

In their anxiety over their brother's health, the women had immediately turned to Jesus, sending him the message: "Lord, the man you love is ill." Jesus had not come immediately and by the time he arrived, Lazarus had been dead in the tomb for four days already.

Following this extract, Jesus commands Lazarus to come out of the tomb and bids those around him to unbind him and let him go free.

The story of the raising of Lazarus comes only in John's Gospel and chronologically as well as in other more significant ways, it is closely related to Christ's own death and resurrection. The other Gospels do record occasions when Jesus raised people from the dead, (Jairus' daughter, the widow's son at Nain), but Lazarus' recall to life is made particularly significant and dramatic by the fact that he had been dead and in the tomb for several days. There was therefore no possibility that he could have simply appeared to be dead. Unlike the examples of the widow's son and Jairus' daughter, this episode offers Jesus the opportunity to speak of death and resurrection in a profound way which helps our understanding of his own imminent death and resurrection.

3. Consider

● the complete trust in Jesus of Mary and Martha. Neither articulates a specific request to Jesus, nor suggests what course of action he should take. The message they send simply tells him the facts, and when they greet him, they merely tell him of their belief that Lazarus would not have died if Jesus had been there.

● the predominance of faith in Martha's approach. As soon as she hears of Jesus' arrival she goes to meet him and even in her grief and disappointment, acknowledges Jesus as the Son of God who has a special relationship with his Father.

● Martha's openness to Jesus and her ready engagement in learning more about his nature and the concept of resurrection. Her initial understanding seems quite remote – "I know he will rise again at the resurrection on the last day", repeating an article of Pharisaic faith which actually gives her little comfort. However, she allows Jesus to lead her on in faith, and ends her conversation with him still puzzled, yet full of trust and a living faith – "I believe that you are the Christ, the Son of God, the one who was to come into this world." This confession of faith stands out as the fullest yet made by any of Jesus' followers.

- Martha's awareness that the new understanding and insights that she has received from Jesus must immediately be shared with her sister.

- Mary has allowed her elder sister, the more active Martha, to reach Jesus first, and has quietly waited inside. When called, she goes to Jesus and throws herself at his feet, weeping.

4. Jesus' response

Jesus' response to each of the sisters is personal and individual. He meets the particular needs of each one fully and sensitively. Recognising Martha's need to understand more fully, and to discuss with him, Jesus rewards her for her faith by sharing with her a profound teaching on the resurrection.

He is moved by Mary's tears and recognises her instinctive, less verbalised puzzlement and grief. It is after her approach that he acts rather than explains. Jesus' response to both women is an empathetic one. He feels with them in their grief, and although he knows that he can give Lazarus back to them, he nevertheless weeps with them.

He recognises their truly human grief, and responds to them on this level by raising Lazarus, as well as leading them on in faith with his discourse on resurrection.

Thus he shows us that the expression of our human emotions is not a matter for repression or shame – nor is grief at death a contradiction of faith.

5. Prayer

Thank God for this most human and loving of all stories – for Jesus' compassionate awareness of the torment of grief, and for the mercy he brings to the situations.

Lay before the Lord those situations that most grieve you. Allow him to be with you as you grieve, and let him raise you up, unbinding you from whatever holds you in this grief.

Make Martha's declaration of faith your own, even in moments when its fullest meaning puzzles you. Learn from these women that God is attentive to your deepest needs without you having to petition him.

Death and Resurrection are central
to your message, Lord.
Help me to grow in my understanding
of them.
I see them all around me:
in nature, in the seasons,
in those I love,
in my own inner life.
Give me faith even when I grieve
and lead me to an even stronger faith in you.
Your Father and your spirit.

THE ANOINTING AT BETHANY

JOHN 12:1-8

Prodigal Waste

Six days before the Passover, Jesus went to Bethany, where Lazarus was, whom he had raised from the dead. They gave a dinner for him there; Martha waited on them and Lazarus was among those at table. Mary brought in a pound of very costly ointment, pure nard, and with it anointed the feet of Jesus, wiping them with her hair; the house was full of the scent of the ointment. Then Judas Iscariot – one of his disciples, the man who was to betray him – said, "Why, wasn't this ointment sold for three hundred denarii, and the money given to the poor?" He said this not because he cared about the poor, but because he was a thief; he was in charge of the common fund and used to help himself to the contributions. So Jesus said, "Leave her alone; she had to keep this scent for the day of my burial. You have the poor with you always, you will not always have me."

1. Read and reread the passage reflectively.

2. Context
This story appears in different forms and in different contexts in each of the Gospels. Matthew, Mark and Luke emphasise different aspects of the story and feature women in different ways.
One thing is very clear, and that is that Jesus recognised the value of the woman's generosity.

3. Consider
● the ointment which Mary of Bethany brings is very costly, is of very good quality and is in abundance: "the house was full of the scent of the ointment".

- Mary has to endure the criticisms of the men around Jesus, including those of the "keeper of the purse" who accuses her of denying the poor charity.

- in her love of Jesus, Mary is not restrained by social conventions or norms. She anoints Jesus' feet – tradition would make this very unusual. She dries his feet with her hair in a culture where respectable Jewish women would not appear in public with their hair unbound.

- Mary's approach is one of mercy. The onlookers are being challenged to treat her with that same mercy.

4. Jesus' response

Jesus turns away Mary's critics and takes her part. He looks at the deeper significance of her action and interprets her generosity as an unconscious preparation of his body for burial, as an expression of great love. In doing so, he acknowledges that her money has been well spent.

5. Prayer

In praying with Mary of Bethany, try to become aware of situations in your own life at the moment where conventions and "social prudence" are restraining your generous response to the Gospel message.

Ask God to give you the strength to respond with lavish generosity to his presence in the world.

*Thank you, Lord, for Mary's
generous and unselfish love
in serving you.
Help me to love you and others
fully, not counting the cost and
without self-interest.
I pray especially for all those
people in the world who
are hungry and in need
in all sorts of ways.
May we who are more fortunate
respond to them with Mary's
unconditional love and generosity.
Help me to become more
sensitive to the need to share the
world's resources more justly.*

THE WOMEN AT THE FOOT OF THE CROSS

JOHN 19:25-27

Spiritual Motherhood

Near the cross of Jesus stood his mother and his mother's sister, Mary the wife of Clopas, Mary of Magdala. Seeing his mother and the disciple he loved standing near her, Jesus said to his mother, "Woman, this is your son." Then to the disciple he said, "This is your mother." And from that moment the disciple made a place for her in his home.

1. Read and reread the passage reflectively.

2. Context

Different accounts of the Way of the Cross and the Crucifixion accord different roles to various individual women and groups of women. Although the details may vary, all four Gospels give a special place of fidelity, love and compassion to women at the end of Jesus' life. St John alone has four women at the foot of the cross – all women who loved Jesus. They are: Mary, Jesus' mother, Mary from Magdala from whom Jesus cast out seven devils, Jesus' mother's sister, and Mary the wife of Clopas, about whom we know nothing.

3. Consider

● the courage of the women who put themselves in this dangerous position. They are expressing their love and support for someone widely regarded as a criminal and a heretic, someone who has been condemned to death by a Roman government and deserving of crucifixion.

● the faith of the women who, almost alone, believe that Jesus is the Messiah right up to his death and burial. Their belief in him has been loyal and constant, quiet and strong.

- the trust of the women. Surrounded by weak or disappointed followers who have lost heart, who have even denied or betrayed Jesus, these women, without question or rebuke, bitterness or resentment, stay at Jesus' side.

- the significance of this scene when Jesus, in agony on his cross, makes a special moment of entrusting his mother to the care of his "beloved disciple".

- in his fully human distress, Jesus believes that he has been abandoned even by his Father. His disciples, other than John, have taken fright, and four women alone keep silent vigil with him to the end.

4. Jesus' response

No response could be expected from this dying man, so cruelly treated by his enemies and rejected by his friends; and yet Jesus saw his mother, and in his filial love and total unselfishness, he addressed her in loving concern.

He uses the word "Woman" ("Gunai"); the same form of address used at the wedding feast of Cana. This implies great and respectful love, and highlights the moment as one of deep intimacy. With gentleness and an appreciation of what his death will mean to both his mother and to his "beloved disciple", he gives to each the care of the other. This loving concern has been the hallmark of his relationships throughout his life.

In terms of Jesus' response to women in the Gospels, this moment is of great significance. At his death, Jesus accords to Mary the highest accolades, as he entrusts John in her keeping. In addressing Mary not as "Mother" but as "Woman", he recognises the true and just place that belongs to women in the future mission of the Church and the salvation of humankind. Linking her to the first woman, Eve, Jesus presents a model of womanhood in leadership, confirming Mary as the spiritual mother of the Church.

5. Prayer

Prayerfully reflect on the qualities that these women show as they wait at the foot of the Cross. Ask God to increase these qualities in you.

Ponder on situations in your life today when you can be present to the suffering of those who have been condemned, rejected, or abandoned: marginalised in some way by a lack of justice in their fellow human beings.

Thank God for the example of these women, and for your insight into their relevance in our world today, where so many are in need of courageous and faithful support.

Father, your son, Jesus,
knew abandonment
and rejection
and it was only a faithful few
who stayed with him to the end.
I pray that I will always be faithful to Jesus
no matter what the cost
as I seek to support those abandoned
and rejected by people today.
May Mary's role as mother of the Church
inspire me to take
an active part in the Church,
witnessing to the death and resurrection of your Son.

THE WOMEN AT THE TOMB

MATTHEW 28:1-10

The Centrality of Women
in the Mission of the Church

After the Sabbath, and towards dawn on the first day of the week, Mary of Magdala and the other Mary went to visit the sepulchre. And all at once there was a violent earthquake, for the angel of the Lord, descending from heaven, came and rolled away the stone and sat on it. His face was like lightening, his robe white as snow. The guards were so shaken, so frightened of him, that they were like dead men. But the angel spoke; and he said to the women, "There is no need for you to be afraid. I know you are looking for Jesus, who was crucified. He is not here, for he has risen, as he said he would. Come and see the place where he lay, then go quickly and tell his disciples, 'He has risen from the dead and now he is going before you to Galilee; it is there you will see him.' Now I have told you." Filled with awe and great joy the women came quickly away from the tomb and ran to tell the disciples.
And there, coming to meet them, was Jesus. "Greetings" he said. And the woman came up to him and, falling down before him, clasped his feet. Then Jesus said to them, "Do not be afraid; go and tell my brothers that they must leave for Galilee; they will see me there."

1. Read and reread the passage reflectively.

2. Context
All four Gospels agree that the primary witnesses to the Resurrection were women. The details differ, but this central fact remains. A fact that would have been unpalatable within the contemporary patriarchal culture. Women not only witness the fact of the Resurrection, but are entrusted with passing on the Good News. They do this quickly and faithfully.

3. Consider

● the events of the previous two days had left the women disappointed and distressed. On the surface there was no reason to hope. Nevertheless they did not give up, and "towards dawn" they are the first to visit the sepulchre.

● the angel recognises the women's faith and confides in them, while the male guards were "like dead men", unable to respond.

● the women respond instinctively and quickly to the angel, recognising the facts of the Resurrection instantly and unquestioningly.

● as they rush away on this the first mission of the new church, they come face to face with Jesus. Despite their excitement and haste, they are open to recognising Jesus, to honouring him and to obeying him.

● the women overcome their fear and immediately trust in the mission given to them directly by Jesus.

● in justice, women are rewarded for their faithfulness to Jesus – faithfulness that found them at the foot of the Cross.

4. Jesus' response

Jesus is quick to reassure the women, acknowledging their significance at this most important of moments. He entrusts them with the most vital news of all time: the Good News of the Resurrection.

He is gentle with them, yet appears to have complete trust that they will carry out their mission fully and faithfully.

5. Prayer

Ponder and pray over this, the greatest moment of endorsement for women in the Gospels.

Reflect on their courage, their love of Jesus and their ability to rise above the disappointments and distress of previous events.

Ask God for the strength not to underestimate the work he has for you as a woman in a culture which still undervalues women's gifts.

Pray for a fuller understanding of your role in continuing the work of these women in spreading the Good News of the Resurrection.

Thank you, Father, for this most
wonderful story of faith and
trust. Help me to believe
that if I put you at the centre
of my life, I can be stronger
and braver in my service
of you and others.
I pray for a fuller understanding
of my role in your mission
in the Church.
May we all be worthy inheritors
of the missionary zeal of those
first women.

CONCLUSION

Spending time in prayer with some of the women of the Gospels, and encountering Christ with them, has perhaps enabled us to extend our understanding of the particular qualities of women, and of the value that Jesus attaches to such qualities. We have literally "stood under" each one and will have experienced something of each woman's distinctive nature as well as the characteristics which are common to them in their femininity.

Particular feminine qualities have become apparent through these texts. There is the intuitive grasp of faith and the desire to share it, which we saw in the Woman with the Haemorrhage, the Crippled Woman and the Woman who had lost her coins. We have seen courageous women who refuse to let themselves be trapped by society's norms and prejudices, evidenced significantly in the Canaanite Woman and the Woman at the Well. Time and again Jesus entrusts his Mission to women, and they are always quick and faithful in their response. The stories of Elizabeth and Mary, and of Mary and Martha have illustrated the importance of recognising and even reverencing difference and complementarity. We have also seen the loving fidelity of those women at the foot of the cross and of the women at the tomb. In these particular cases we can see plainly God's affirmation as he chooses women to be with his Son at his death and to be the first witnesses of the Resurrection. At the outset it was noted that whilst the culture and the time gave little significance to women, seeing them merely as subservient, Jesus gave them a recognition that was out of the ordinary. Indeed his attitude points to a restoration of God's original plan for them.

If we read on in the New Testament we find, predominantly in the Acts of the Apostles, but also in Paul's Letters, women amongst those at the heart of the early Christian Church. There is Tabitha, Lydia, Mary the mother of John Mark. There are several wives who appear to have a role in their own right: Sapphira, Priscilla, Druscilla. All these women, and several others, merit our reflection and show that the early Christian Church gave women a place that they had in no other area of their society. Jesus had recognised in women those qualities needed in mission. The women of Acts were the inheritors of that missionary task first entrusted to the women at the tomb. We too are entrusted with that same mission in our own time. Far from being a task just for women, the work of mission is a work for all Christians, men and women, but it calls out for the feminine in each of us.

Our meditations on some of the women in the Gospels may have led us to consider the notion of the necessary complementarity of the male and the female – necessary both in terms of God's desire for the world and in terms of the healthy functioning of any society. In our post-modernist world we see the escalation of the breakdown of relationships: both between individuals and on a global scale. Many would argue that one of the significant causes of this is the primacy of such predominantly masculine characteristics as reason, order, control. Complementarity requires that human balance be restored by the feminine values which we have encountered being recognised and given their rightful place. It tells us that there IS another way. This way will free both men and women to be their full and most human selves, and will bring to relationships on all levels, from those of a personal, intimate nature through to those with out environment, a God-like quality.

The Trinity integrates within itself all that is best in us creatures, created in the image and likeness of our God. In its earliest days, Christianity seemed to be growing into a model of this integration, with its recognition of the need for a Church which values equally the qualities of both the male and the female – a Church which would recognise that such wholeness should be the aim of our striving for ourselves, for our society and for our world. Many women have been, in turn the focus of our prayer and we have continually noted Jesus' loving affirmation of the qualities of their lives and especially of their faith.

The Resurrection is the centre, the high point of the Good News. It is significant that women were chosen as the primary witnesses of this event. Loving women were with Jesus through to his death on the cross and women were there to greet him as he overcame death. Women were given the essential message, that Good News of our liberation and of our ultimate fullness of life with God. They, and therefore we, were given the task of spreading that "Good News". The Resurrection, in so many different ways, turns our world upside down. It reverses patterns, upends assumptions. It challenges us to do the same. It challenges us, as it challenged those women who witnessed it, to leave behind much of what we cling on to and instead to live in the embrace of justice and mercy.